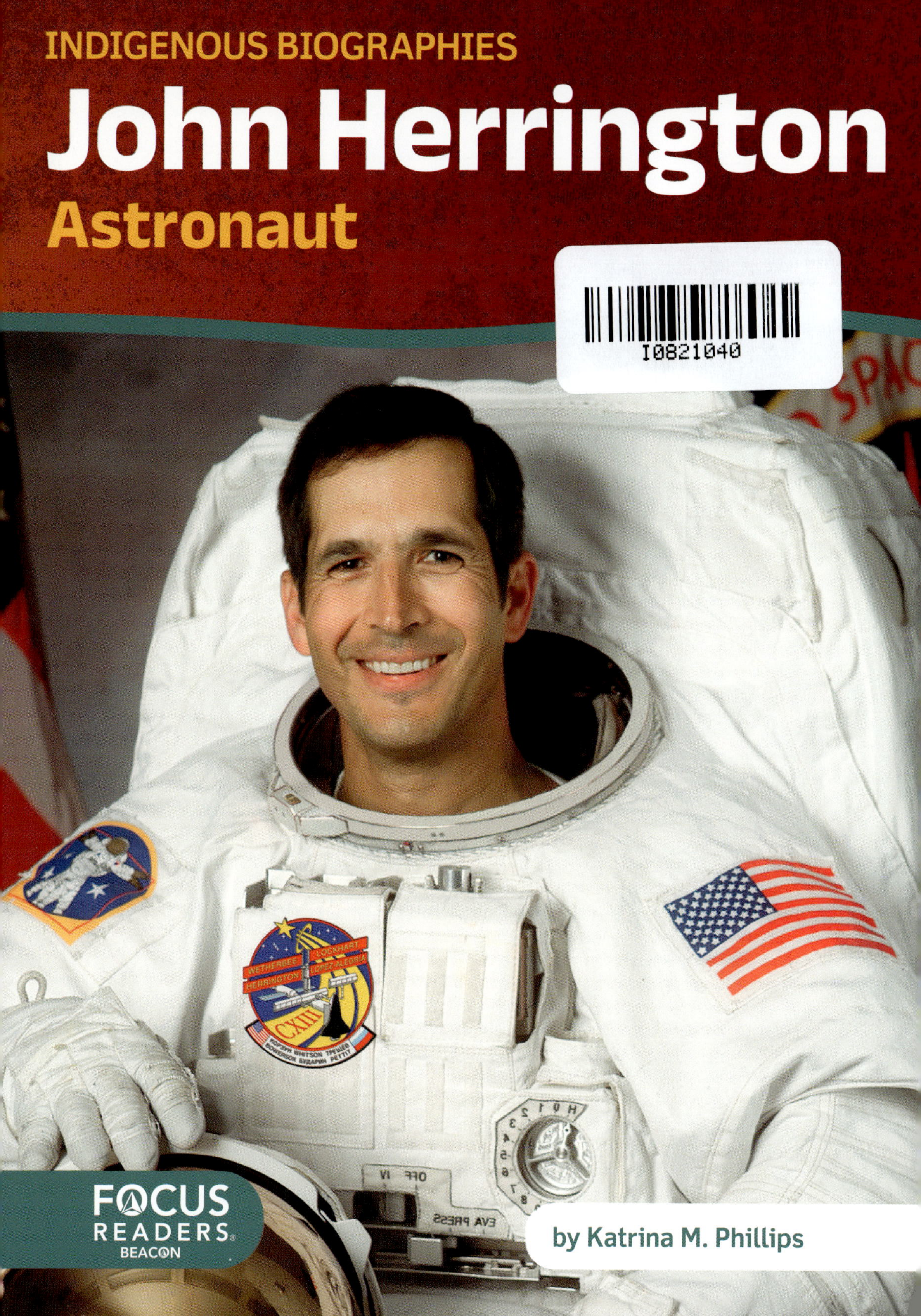
INDIGENOUS BIOGRAPHIES
John Herrington
Astronaut
I0821040
WETHERBEE
LOCKHART
HERRINGTON
LOPEZ-ALEGRIA
CXIII
FOCUS READERS
BEACON
by Katrina M. Phillips

www.focusreaders.com

Focus Readers is distributed by North Star Editions:
sales@northstareditions.com | 888-417-0195

Produced for Focus Readers by Red Line Editorial.

Photographs ©: David DeHoyos/NASA, cover, 1; NASA, 4, 7, 14, 16, 19, 22, 29; Timothy Swope/Alamy, 8; Jeff Zehnder/Alamy, 11; Shutterstock Images, 13, 27; iStockphoto, 21; Sue Ogrocki/AP Images, 24

Library of Congress Cataloging-in-Publication Data
Names: Phillips, Katrina M. author
Title: John Herrington: astronaut / by Katrina M. Phillips.
Description: Mendota Heights, MN: Focus Readers, [2026] | Series: Indigenous biographies | Includes bibliographical references and index. | Audience: Grades 2-3
Identifiers: LCCN 2025015356 (print) | LCCN 2025015357 (ebook) | ISBN 9798889985020 hardcover | ISBN 9798889986560 paperback | ISBN 9798889985655 pdf | ISBN 9798889985341 ebook
Subjects: LCSH: Herrington, John B. (John Bennett), 1958---Juvenile literature | Indian astronauts--Biography--Juvenile literature | Chickasaw Indians--Biography--Juvenile literature | LCGFT: Literature. | Biographies.
Classification: LCC E99.C55 P485 2026 (print) | LCC E99.C55 (ebook) | DDC 629.450092 [B]--dc23/eng/20250424
LC record available at https://lccn.loc.gov/2025015356
LC ebook record available at https://lccn.loc.gov/2025015357

Printed in the United States of America
Mankato, MN
012026

About the Author

Dr. Katrina M. Phillips (Red Cliff Ojibwe) is a writer, researcher, and history professor. She's written several children's books about Native histories and cultures, including *Indigenous Peoples' Day* and *I Am on Indigenous Land*. She and her husband live in Minnesota with their two sons and their goofy dog.

Table of Contents

WETHERBEE

CHAPTER 1

Out of This World

John Herrington made history in 2002. But it didn't happen here on Earth. Herrington became the first enrolled member of a Native nation to go into space. He was a citizen of the Chickasaw Nation.

John Herrington spent more than 330 hours in space.

Herrington was an astronaut for **NASA**. He flew to the **International Space Station** (ISS). The mission lasted nearly two weeks.

Herrington took several things with him. He brought an eagle feather. He carried a braid of **sweetgrass**. He also had his

Did You Know?

Herrington completed three **space walks** during the mission. He was the 143rd person to walk in space.

Herrington was the first Native astronaut to do a space walk.

traditional flute. These were all important to his Native **culture**. Herrington brought the flag of the Chickasaw Nation, too.

PolyPro
Bank

CHAPTER 2

Joining the Navy

John Herrington was born in Wetumka, Oklahoma, on September 14, 1958. His father served in the military. John's family moved a lot when he was a kid.

When John Herrington was growing up, he spent time living in Riverton, Wyoming.

He grew up in Colorado, Wyoming, and Texas.

John liked to set up little rockets with his brother and their dad. He loved pretending a cardboard box was a rocket ship on its way to the moon. Both of John's parents also loved to fly. His dad worked as a

Did You Know?

John's family moved 14 times before he finished high school.

Herrington received his college degree in Colorado Springs, Colorado.

flight instructor. John took his first flying lesson from his dad.

In college, Herrington studied how to use math to solve real-world problems. He also had a job helping other students in a math class.

One of those students had been a pilot in the US Navy. That student got Herrington interested in flying again. Herrington finished college in 1983. Soon after, he joined the Navy. He became a pilot in 1985.

In 1990, Herrington took another step in his career. He became a test pilot for the Navy. He flew new aircraft to test how well they worked.

Herrington learned that many astronauts had started out as

As a test pilot, Herrington tested a P-3 Orion. That is a type of spy plane.

test pilots. He realized he could be an astronaut, too. So, he earned a degree in **aeronautical engineering**. Herrington thought the education would help him reach his goal.

NASA
JOHN B. HERRINGTON

CHAPTER 3

Heading to Space

John Herrington was invited to join NASA in 1996. More than 2,500 people had applied to be an astronaut. Herrington was one of only 44 who were picked. He spent several years training.

John Herrington was part of the 16th class of NASA astronauts.

Then Herrington got his first flight assignment. He helped prepare for the launch and landing.

Herrington's turn to go to space finally came in 2002. Before his mission, NASA held an event to celebrate him. People from more than 45 Native nations came. The event included Native dances and Native music. It showed the difference Herrington had made. He had helped make science and space more **accessible** for Native people.

***Endeavour* launches into space on November 23, 2002.**

Herrington left Earth in November 2002. He flew in the space shuttle *Endeavour*. Herrington and the other astronauts had many jobs. They carried supplies for the ISS.

They helped install a new piece on the station. The mission also delivered a new crew of astronauts. It brought the old crew back to Earth.

Herrington had made history. To honor his journey, he donated

Did You Know?

In 2022, Nicole Aunapu Mann became the first Native woman in space. She is a citizen of the Wailacki Tribe. This tribe is part of the Round Valley Indian Tribes.

Nicole Aunapu Mann went to the ISS as part of the Crew-5 mission.

his flute and eagle feather to the National Museum of the American Indian in Washington, DC.

TOPIC SPOTLIGHT

Native Knowledge

Indigenous nations have always looked to the stars. The Diné call one group of stars the Thunderbird. It is first seen in early spring. That's around the time thunderstorms become more common. The Očhéthi Šakówiŋ, or Seven Council Fires, call the Milky Way *Wanáǧi Thačhankú*. This means the "Road of the Spirits."

Around a thousand years ago, the people of Cahokia built a place called Monks Mound. At its base, it was bigger than the pyramids in Egypt. They built Monks Mound based on the way the stars, sun, and moon moved.

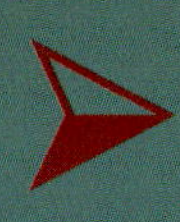

The Ojibwe call the Northern Lights *Jiibayag Niimi'idiway*. *Jiibayag* means "spirit." *Niimi'idiway* means "they dance."

CHAPTER 4

Back on Earth

John Herrington **retired** from the Navy and NASA in 2005. But he kept busy. In 2008, he biked across the United States. He rode 4,000 miles (6,400 km) through 11 states.

Before retiring, John Herrington tested extreme environments on Earth that were similar to space.

Herrington has led many classes for young people about space and science.

Along the way, Herrington stopped at many schools. He wanted to inspire students who were interested in science, technology, engineering, and math. He called the bike ride "Rocketrek."

Herrington continued to travel the country. And he kept teaching people about space travel. He talked to Native children and young adults about math and science.

Did You Know?

In 2016, Herrington wrote a book for children. The book is called *Mission to Space*. It shows his journey to becoming an astronaut.

Herrington also went back to school. He began attending the University of Idaho. In 2014, he earned a PhD in education.

Herrington received many honors for his work. In 2017, he was inducted into the International Air & Space Hall of Fame. The next year, he was chosen for the National Native American Hall of Fame. He was one of the first people to earn that honor. In 2019, the United States released a special dollar

The International Air & Space Hall of Fame is located in the San Diego Air & Space Museum.

coin. It celebrated his space walk. Herrington had always dreamed of going to space. His dream came true. He wanted to help others reach their goals, too.

Focus Questions

Write your answers on a separate piece of paper.

1. Write a letter to a friend about John Herrington's trip to space.
2. Would you like to go to outer space? Why or why not?
3. When did John Herrington go to space?
   - **A.** 1996
   - **B.** 2002
   - **C.** 2014
4. Why did Herrington think a degree in aeronautical engineering would help him become an astronaut?
   - **A.** All test pilots needed the degree to be hired.
   - **B.** The degree would let him fly aircraft for the first time.
   - **C.** NASA would know he had enough education and skills.

5. What does **enrolled** mean in this book?

Herrington became the first ***enrolled*** *member of a Native nation to go into space. He was a citizen of the Chickasaw Nation.*

A. astronaut
B. official
C. child

6. What does **inducted** mean in this book?

In 2017, he was ***inducted*** *into the International Air & Space Hall of Fame. The next year, he was chosen for the National Native American Hall of Fame.*

A. added to a group
B. fired from a job
C. removed from an event

Answer key on page 32.

Glossary

accessible
Easily able to be understood, appreciated, or participated in.

aeronautical engineering
A field that uses math and science to work on aircraft.

culture
The customs, arts, beliefs, and laws of a group of people.

Indigenous
Native to a region, or belonging to ancestors who lived in a region before colonists arrived.

International Space Station
A large spacecraft that orbits Earth. It serves as a home for astronauts and a science lab.

NASA
The National Aeronautics and Space Administration, a part of the US government that focuses on space research and travel.

retired
Left a job or career.

space walks
When astronauts go outside spacecraft and move around in space.

sweetgrass
A plant with important uses for many Native nations.

To Learn More

BOOKS

Gagne, Tammy. *John Herrington: First Native American in Space*. Mitchell Lane Publishers, 2024.

Herrington, John. *Mission to Space*. Chickasaw Press, 2016.

Stratton, Connor. *Space Exploration*. Focus Readers, 2023.

NOTE TO EDUCATORS

Visit **www.focusreaders.com** to find links and resources related to this title.

Index

Answer Key: 1. Answers will vary; 2. Answers will vary; 3. B; 4. C; 5. B; 6. A